THE LEMON & LIME COOKBOOK

THE
LEMON & LIME
COOKBOOK

hamlyn

First published in 2000
by Hamlyn
an imprint of Octopus Publishing Group Limited
2–4 Heron Quays, London E14 4JP

ISBN 0 600 60068 8

Printed in China

Photographer: Ian Wallace
Home Economist: Susie Theodorou

NOTES

1 The American Egg Board advises that eggs should not be consumed raw. This book contains some dishes made with raw or lightly cooked eggs. It is prudent for more vulnerable people such as pregnant and nursing mothers, invalids, the elderly, babies, and young children to avoid uncooked or lightly cooked dishes made with eggs.

2 Meat and poultry should be cooked thoroughly. To test if poultry is cooked, pierce the flesh through the thickest part with a skewer or fork—the juices should run clear, never pink or red. Keep refrigerated until ready for cooking.

3 This book includes dishes made with nuts and nut derivatives. It is advisable for those with known allergic reactions to nuts and nut derivatives and those who may be potentially vulnerable to these allergies, such as pregnant and nursing mothers, invalids, the elderly, babies, and children, to avoid dishes made with nuts and nut oils. It is also prudent to check the labels of prepreared ingredients for the possible inclusion of nut derivatives.

Contents

THE LEMON & LIME COOKBOOK

Lemons are one of the most indispensable ingredients in the cook's repertoire. They are used at every course, from appetizers through main course dishes to desserts, they add an inimitable flavor to cakes and cookies, and a whole range of marinades, dressings, and sauces would hardly be the same without them. For serious cooks, scarcely a day goes by when a dish isn't enhanced by a squeeze of lemon juice. Home-made lemonade and iced mint tea are the ideal thirst quenchers on a hot summer's day; indeed soft drinks and cocktails are also where the lime comes into its own—think in particular of the Margarita and the Cuba Libre (see page 62).

The roll call of famous lemon and lime dishes is extensive, ranging from Avgolemono, a light soup flavored with eggs and lemon juice (see page 12), to Tahitian Limed Fish (see page 40), in which the fish is 'cooked' by soaking in a lime juice marinade, a technique which is also used in the Mexican dish ceviche. Chicken has an affinity with lemon, and dishes using lemon with chicken are found all around the world, with subtle, national variations, with lime taking the place of lemon in tropical recipes. Desserts include the classic lemon meringue pie, lemon tarts from France, lime meringue pie from the United States, and granitas and sorbets from Italy, the home of the world's most delectable ices. In addition, candied lemon and lime slices and julienne zest strips make an attractive decoration for cakes and cold desserts. And, of course, there is marmalade from Britain, without which breakfast is incomplete, as well as preserved lemons from North Africa, the peel chopped and used in savory dishes, and lemon curd from Scotland. Lemon and lime juice can be used to sharpen the flavor of food for those on a low salt or salt-free diet.

History

Lemons and limes both originated somewhere in Southeast Asia. Lemons have been cultivated for over 2000 years and are thought to have reached Europe sometime during the 1st century AD. During the middle ages cultivation was established around the Mediterranean and Crusaders returning from Palestine brought these rare fruits to Britain in the 13th century. In Christian symbolism a lemon was an emblem of fidelity in love, and there are examples in Italian Renaissance paintings of the infant Jesus being given lemons, although fruit was considered unsuitable for children at that time. Lemons were a great luxury in those days. To celebrate the coronation of Anne Boleyn in 1533 the Leatherseller's Company of the City of London gave a great feast for Henry VIII and his new queen and paid six silver pennies to buy a single lemon for the occasion. Lemon groves were established in the Azores by 1494, and these coveted fruits reached the Americas at the end of the 15th century when Christopher Columbus took citrus fruit seed with him to the West Indies on his second voyage in 1493.

In the 15th and 16th centuries, ships usually set out for long voyages in the spring, but their crews were frequently very rundown after a winter without fresh fruit or vegetables and soon became victims of scurvy, the debilitating disease caused by vitamin C deficiency. By the beginning of the 17th century western medical men had established that eating citrus fruit was a cure for scurvy. One hundred years later, at the end of the 18th century, the British Admiralty decreed that a regular quantity of lemon juice should be given every day to sailors after 5–6 weeks at sea. It was usually mixed with the rum ration and must have been the high spot of their day. In the mid–19th century limes were planted on a large scale in the West Indies and were substituted for lemons by the Royal and Merchant Navies, but proved a less effective remedy, as they are lower in vitamin C.

Cultivation

Lemons grow best in subtropical countries while limes flourish in the tropics. Both the lemon and the lime ripen on the tree and do not develop after they are picked. Lemons are cultivated worldwide, with California and Italy providing an especially favorable environment. Other major lemon producers include Israel, Spain, Portugal, Greece, Cyprus, northern and southern Africa, Australia, Argentina and Chile. The lemon trees are usually planted in orchards where they bloom throughout the year and the fruit is picked 6–10 times annually.

The lemon has an acid juicy pulp and an aromatic yellow rind. The outer layer, the zest, is where the aromatic citrus oil and most of the vitamins are concentrated. Lemons may have a thin smooth skin or a thick knobbly one; smooth skinned lemons contain the most juice, knobbly ones have more peel. When buying lemons, choose heavy fragrant ones with a moist-looking lemon yellow skin. A shrivelled skin means that some of the juice may already have begun to evaporate. Lemons can be stored in the refrigerator for 1 month. When possible add lemon juice to dishes after cooking as the vitamin C content disappears on heating.

The lime has a bright green skin and a very sour pulp; it is smaller than the lemon, about the size of a golf ball, and more fragrant and juicy. Limes are grown in tropical regions, among them Brazil, Mexico, the West Indies, and Florida; they are the most perishable of all citrus fruit and will keep only for 1 week in the refrigerator. Although limes can be used in the same way as lemons bear in mind that the flavor is different, limes being stronger and more sour. To interchange lime and lemon juice in recipes, double the quantity of lemon juice and halve the quantity of lime juice.

Zest

Buy lemons or limes with untreated skins if you want to pare or grate the zest. If you can't get untreated fruit, scrub the lemons or limes well in hot water then rinse and dry them thoroughly before use. Use a zester if your recipe asks for the zest of a lemon or lime and

chop the zest if necessary. This is much more effective than using the small holes on a box grater. A canelle knife is the ideal implement if you want long strips of lemon or lime zest to decorate drinks or desserts. Both the zester and the canelle knife remove just the zest and leave the bitter pith behind. Older recipes sometimes ask you to rub sugar lumps over the skin of the lemon to release the essential oil of the zest. To do this, you will need about 4 sugar lumps to each lemon.

Juice

Cut the lemon or lime in half and squeeze it with a lemon squeezer. Manual lemon squeezers can be made of glass, stainless steel or plastic; the most effective ones consist of a reamer mounted on a container that collects the juice. Wooden reamers with a short handle are very efficient both for extracting small quantities of juice and for forcing the very last drops of juice out of a lemon or lime. Always squeeze your own lemon or lime juice for recipes. You will find that it is infinitely superior to the bottled version.

Hints and Tips

To extract the maximum amount of juice from a lemon or lime, warm whole fruits in a moderate oven for a couple of minutes or roll them firmly over a hard surface.

Should you need to revive a lemon which is past its prime, soak it for about 30 minutes in a bowl of hot water.

If you only need a few drops of lemon or lime juice, pierce the fruit with a fine skewer or a darning needle to save cutting it. This means that the lemon or lime can be saved and more of the juice used again at a later stage.

To cut lemons, or other citrus fruit into segments, first remove the zest and pith. Slide the knife down one side of each segment, cutting it away from the skin, then cut down the other side of the skin and lift out the segment. Continue in this way around the lemon.

When serving lemon quarters or wedges with fish, always slice the lemons lengthwise. Pierce the quarter or wedge with a fork so that when you squeeze the lemon the juice falls directly on to the food.

Adding a squeeze of citrus juice to your bowl of water when preparing fruit and vegetables such as apples and pears, Jerusalem artichokes, and celeriac helps to prevent discoloration. Lemon juice can also be brushed directly on to halved or sliced fruit or vegetables to prevent discoloration.

A little grated lemon zest adds piquancy to bread and rice-based stuffings for roast meat.

Follow the Italian example and use lemon juice instead of vinegar in salad dressings. It gives a fresher and softer finish.

To make decorative lemon and lime slices, use a canelle knife to remove strips of the zest at intervals along the length of the fruit, then cut the fruit into slices.

To make lemon and lime twists, slice the fruit thinly then make a cut from the center to the edge. Twist the two sides of the slit in opposite directions so that the twist will stand up.

Halve lemons and scrape out the pulp and membranes, then use the shells as containers to serve ice creams, sorbets or granitas.

Preserved Lemons

To preserve lemons, put 2 teaspoons of coarse salt in a sterilized preserving jar. Using a sharp knife, cut the lemon lengthwise as if about to quarter it, but do not cut quite through. Ease out any pits.

Pack 1 tablespoon of salt into the cuts, then close them and place in the jar. Repeat with more lemons, packing them tightly, until the jar is full. Squeeze another lemon and pour the juice over the fruit. Sprinkle with more coarse salt and top up with boiling water to cover the lemons.

Close the jar tightly and keep it in a warmish place for about 3–4 weeks. Do not worry if, on longer storage, a lacy white film appears on top of the jar or on the preserved lemons; it is quite harmless—simply rinse it off.

Stock Recipes

A number of recipes in this book require chicken or vegetable stock. It is always better to use a home-made stock rather than a bought one. Make a substantial amount at one time, then use what you need for the recipe and freeze the remainder in freezer containers or ice cube trays.

Chicken Stock

1 chicken carcass, raw or cooked
1 onion, roughly chopped
2 large carrots
1 celery stalk
1 bay leaf
a few parsley stalks
1 thyme sprig
3 pints cold water

1 Chop the chicken carcass into 3 or 4 pieces and put in a large, heavy-based saucepan with any trimmings. Add the onion, carrots, celery, and bay leaf. Crush the parsley stalks lightly and add them, with the thyme. Pour over the water to cover.
2 Bring the stock to the boil, skimming off any scum that rises to the surface. Cover the pan and simmer for 2–2½ hours.
3 Strain the stock through a muslin-lined sieve and leave to cool before putting in the refrigerator. If the stock is to be frozen, cool it quickly (sit the bowl of stock in cold water, for instance) first.

Makes 1¾ pints
Preparation time: 15 minutes
Cooking time: about 2¾ hours

Vegetable Stock

1 pound mixed vegetables, chopped
1 garlic clove
1 bouquet garni (2 parsley sprigs, 2 thyme sprigs, 2 bay leaves)
2 pints cold water

1 Put the vegetables, garlic, and bouquet garni in a large, heavy-based saucepan. Pour over the water.
2 Bring the stock to the boil, cover the saucepan and simmer gently for 30 minutes, skimming off any scum that rises to the surface.
3 Strain the stock, and cool before storing in the refrigerator, until it is needed.

Makes 1¾ pints
Preparation time: 10 minutes
Cooking time: about 45 minutes

AVGOLEMONO

3¾ cups Chicken Stock (see page 10)
⅓ cup long-grain white rice
2 eggs
2–3 tablespoons lemon juice
salt and pepper
1 tablespoon chopped parsley, to garnish
(optional)

1 Combine the stock, ½ teaspoon of salt, and rice in a saucepan. Bring the mixture to a boil. Stir, lower the heat, cover the pan, and simmer for 10–12 minutes. Stir once more.

2 Beat the eggs in a small bowl, then beat in the lemon juice. Add a ladleful of stock, beat the mixture, then add another ladleful of stock and beat again.

3 Bring the remaining stock and the rice mixture to a boil. Briefly remove the pan from the heat and add the egg and lemon mixture. Stir well, then lower the heat, and simmer for a further 2 minutes, adding salt and pepper to taste. Sprinkle with the parsley, if liked. Serve immediately.

Serves 4–6
Preparation time: about 10 minutes
Cooking time: about 15 minutes

HERBED TOMATO AND LEMON BROTH

14–ounce can plum tomatoes
2 tablespoons butter or margarine
**2½ cups Chicken or Vegetable Stock
(see page 10)**
2 tablespoons lemon juice
1 teaspoon grated lemon zest
pepper
½ teaspoon sugar
**4 drops of Tabasco or hot pepper sauce,
or to taste**
2 teaspoons Worcestershire sauce
1 tablespoon chopped oregano
1 tablespoon chopped parsley
4 thin lemon slices, to garnish

1 Drain the canned tomatoes, reserving half of the juice. Melt the butter or margarine in a saucepan, add the tomatoes, and cook for 5 minutes over a moderate heat, stirring and breaking them up with a wooden spoon.

2 Add the reserved tomato juice, stock, lemon juice and zest, and plenty of pepper to taste. Stir in the sugar, Tabasco or hot pepper sauce, and Worcestershire sauce. Bring the liquid to a boil, then lower the heat and simmer, uncovered, for 15 minutes.

3 Stir in the oregano and parsley and simmer the soup for a further 5 minutes.

4 Remove the soup from the heat and press it through a fine sieve into a clean pan. Heat briefly, if necessary. Serve immediately, garnishing each portion with a lemon slice.

Serves 4
Preparation time: 5 minutes
Cooking time: 30 minutes

DUCK SALAD WITH LIME

¼ roast duck
6 small green chiles, finely sliced
½ red onion, finely sliced
I cup finely chopped cilantro
4 cherry tomatoes, cut into quarters
juice of 2 limes
I teaspoon jaggery or light brown sugar
I½ tablespoons fish sauce (nam pla)
lettuce leaves, to serve

To garnish:
lime wedges
mint leaves

I Skin the duck, if liked, remove the meat, and cut it into small pieces.

2 Heat a wok and then turn the heat off. Put the duck into the wok to warm it through, then add all the remaining ingredients, stirring and turning them thoroughly for 3 minutes.

3 To serve, arrange the lettuce leaves on 4 plates and place the duck salad over them. Garnish with lime wedges and mint leaves.

Serves 4
Preparation time: 8–10 minutes
Cooking time: 5 minutes

TROPICAL LEMON RICE AND WILD RICE SALAD

⅓ cup wild rice, rinsed
1⅓ cups long-grain rice, rinsed
2 tablespoons lemon juice
1 teaspoon sugar
1 teaspoon salt
1 small papaya
1 bunch scallions, sliced
¼ cup toasted and chopped pecan nuts
¼ cup toasted and chopped brazil nuts
¼ cup toasted sunflower seeds
1 tablespoon poppy seeds

Citrus dressing:
6 tablespoons extra virgin olive oil
1 tablespoon lemon juice or lime juice
2 tablespoons chopped parsley
salt and pepper

1 Cook the wild rice in plenty of lightly salted, boiling water for 35 minutes until tender.

2 Meanwhile, put the long-grain rice in a pan with plenty of cold water, add the lemon juice, sugar, and salt, bring to a boil, and simmer gently for 10–12 minutes or until cooked.

3 Drain both the wild and long-grain rices and place in a large bowl. Blend all the dressing ingredients together, season with salt and pepper, and toss with the rice. Set aside until cold.

4 Just before serving, cut the papaya in half, discard the seeds, and peel and dice the flesh. Add to the rice with the scallions, nuts, and seeds. Taste and adjust the seasoning, if necessary, and serve immediately.

Serves 6
Preparation time: 15 minutes, plus cooling
Cooking time: 35 minutes

ZUCCHINI SALAD WITH LEMON AND THYME

1 pound small zucchini
about 16 black olives

Dressing:
5 tablespoons extra virgin olive oil
pared zest of 1 lemon, cut into thin strips
⅓ cup lemon juice
1 garlic clove, crushed
1 tablespoon roughly chopped fresh thyme
1 tablespoon clear honey
salt and pepper

1 To make the dressing, whisk all the ingredients together in a small bowl or place in a screw-top jar, close the lid tightly and shake to combine.
2 Cut the zucchini in half crosswise.
3 Bring a saucepan of water to the boil, add the zucchini and cook for 2 minutes. Drain immediately, blot the excess moisture with paper towels and transfer to a serving bowl. Add the olives.
4 Pour the dressing over the warm zucchini, toss lightly and leave until cold before serving.

Serves 4–6
Preparation time: 20 minutes, plus standing
Cooking time: 2 minutes

GRILLED CORN WITH SPICY SESAME-LIME BUTTER

3 small corn-on-the-cobs
I tablespoon sesame seeds
4 tablespoons unsalted butter, softened
I small red chile, seeded and finely chopped
grated zest and juice of ½–I lime
salt and pepper
watercress sprigs, to serve
grated lime zest, to garnish

I To make the butter, fry the sesame seeds in a small pan with no oil until golden. Allow the sesame seeds to cool slightly and place in a food processor or blender with the butter, chile, grated zest and juice of the lime. Season with salt and pepper to taste. Blend until combined. Transfer the butter to a piece of foil and roll into a sausage shape. Chill for 30 minutes.

2 Preheat the grill pan to moderate. Using a large sharp knife, cut the corn into ½-inch slices. Remove the butter from the foil and cut it into thin slices. Top the corn slices with the butter. Place on the grill pan and cook for 10–12 minutes, turning often and adding more butter as needed until golden and tender. Serve immediately with more butter slices and watercress sprigs and garnish with lime zest.

Serves 6
Preparation time: 15 minutes, plus chilling
Cooking time: 15 minutes

LEMON AND BASIL PENNE

2 garlic cloves, crushed
large handful of basil leaves
5 tablespoons olive oil
zest and juice of 2 lemons
1½ cups dried penne
¾ cup freshly grated Parmesan cheese
salt and pepper

1 Bring a large saucepan of water to a boil.
2 Using a pestle and mortar or a food processor, blend the garlic, basil, olive oil, and lemon zest and juice until smooth.
3 Place the penne in the boiling water and cook for 6–8 minutes, or according to package instructions.
4 Add the Parmesan to the basil mixture, blend well, and season with salt and pepper to taste.
5 Drain the penne thoroughly. Add the pesto and mix well so that the sauce is distributed evenly throughout the penne. Serve immediately.

Serves 4
Preparation time: 10 minutes
Cooking time: 6–8 minutes

SPINACH WITH OLIVE OIL AND LEMON DRESSING

1¼ pounds fresh spinach leaves
2 tablespoons butter
2 garlic cloves, finely chopped
4 tablespoons olive oil
2 tablespoons lemon juice
salt and pepper

1 Wash the spinach in a colander and shake off the excess water. Put the spinach in a large saucepan, sprinkling the layers with a little salt. Cover the pan and cook over a medium heat for 5–7 minutes until the spinach has wilted and is tender, shaking the pan vigorously from time to time.

2 Drain the spinach thoroughly in the colander, then return it to a clean pan and toss over a high heat until no water remains. Add the butter and garlic and continue tossing until combined with the spinach.

3 Turn the spinach into a serving dish. Drizzle over the oil and lemon juice and season with salt and pepper to taste.

Serves 4–6
Preparation time: 5 minutes
Cooking time: 9–10 minutes

SPINACH AND LEMON RISOTTO

4 cups Chicken or Vegetable Stock
(see page 10)
8 tablespoons butter
1 tablespoon olive oil
2 shallots, finely chopped
1½ cups arborio rice
1 pound fresh baby spinach leaves, washed
grated zest and juice of 1 lemon
⅔ cup freshly grated Parmesan cheese
salt and pepper
grated lemon zest, to garnish (optional)

1 Heat the stock in a saucepan to a gentle simmer.

2 Melt 2 tablespoons of the butter and the olive oil in a saucepan, add the shallots, and sauté for 3 minutes.

3 Add the rice and stir well to coat the grains thoroughly with butter and oil. Add a ladleful of stock, enough to cover the rice, and stir well. Simmer gently and continue to stir as frequently as possible, adding more stock as it is absorbed.

4 Before you add the last amount of the stock, stir in the chopped spinach and lemon zest and juice. Season with salt and pepper to taste. Increase the heat, stir well, then add the remaining stock and butter. Cook for a few minutes, then add the grated Parmesan and mix in well. Serve garnished with black pepper and grated lemon zest, if liked.

Serves 4
Preparation time: 5 minutes
Cooking time: 20 minutes

ROAST LEMON CHICKEN

4 tablespoons butter
2 tablespoons grated lemon zest
3 tablespoons lemon juice
4 pound roasting chicken
salt and pepper
lemon slices, to garnish

1 Preheat the oven to 400°F.

2 Cream the butter with the grated lemon zest. Gradually add 1 tablespoon of the lemon juice, then season with salt and pepper. Carefully loosen the skin of the chicken from the flesh without piercing the skin.

3 Spread two-thirds of the butter mixture under the skin, smoothing the skin to spread it evenly. Truss the chicken and rub with the remaining butter mixture.

4 Place the chicken on a roasting pan, breast-side down, and roast for 20 minutes. Turn the chicken, without breaking the skin, breast-side up, and sprinkle with the remaining lemon juice. Continue to cook, basting with the pan juices every 20 minutes, for about 1¼ hours or until the juices run clear when the thigh is pierced with a skewer. Let the chicken rest for 15 minutes, then transfer to a warmed plate and garnish with lemon slices.

Serves 6
Preparation time: 15 minutes, plus resting
Cooking time: 1½ hours

STIR-FRIED LEMON AND SOY CHICKEN

1 egg white
2 teaspoons cornstarch
pinch of salt
2 boneless, skinless chicken breasts,
about 5 ounces each, cut into thin strips
across the grain
1¼ cups vegetable oil, for frying
½ bunch scallions, shredded
1 garlic clove, crushed
lemon slices, to garnish

Lemon and soy sauce:
2 teaspoons cornstarch
4 tablespoons cold Chicken Stock
(see page 10) or water
finely grated zest of ½ lemon
2 tablespoons lemon juice
1 tablespoon soy sauce
2 teaspoons rice wine or dry sherry
2 teaspoons sugar

1 To prepare the sauce, mix the cornstarch with the stock or water to form a thin paste, then stir in the remaining sauce ingredients. Set aside.
2 Lightly beat the egg white, cornstarch, and salt in a shallow dish. Add the strips of chicken and turn to coat. Set aside.
3 Heat a wok until hot. Add the oil and heat over a moderate heat until hot. One at a time, lift the strips of chicken out of the egg white mixture with a fork and drop them into the hot oil. Fry in batches for 3–4 minutes at a time or until golden. Using a slotted spoon, transfer the chicken strips to paper towels to drain. Keep hot.
4 Pour off all but 1 tablespoon of oil from the wok. Add the scallions and garlic and stir-fry over a moderate heat for about 30 seconds. Stir the sauce to mix, pour it into the wok, increase the heat to high, and bring to a boil, stirring constantly.
5 Return the chicken to the wok and stir-fry for 1–2 minutes or until evenly coated in the sauce. Serve immediately, garnished with lemon slices.

Serves 2
Preparation time: 10 minutes
Cooking time: 15 minutes

CHICKEN WITH OLIVES AND PRESERVED LEMONS

2 tablespoons olive oil
I Spanish onion, finely chopped
3 garlic cloves
I teaspoon ground ginger
1½ teaspoons ground cinnamon
large pinch of saffron threads, toasted and crushed
3½ pound stewing chicken
3 cups Chicken Stock (see page 10)
I cup large black olives, rinsed, and soaked, if liked
I Preserved Lemon (see page 10), chopped
large bunch cilantro, finely chopped
large bunch parsley, finely chopped
salt and pepper
couscous, to serve (optional)

I Heat the oil in a skillet, add the onion, and fry gently, stirring frequently until softened and golden.
2 Meanwhile, using a pestle and mortar, crush the garlic with a pinch of salt, then work in the ginger, cinnamon, saffron, and a little pepper. Stir into the onions, cook until fragrant, then remove from the pan and spread over the chicken.
3 Put the chicken into a heavy saucepan or flameproof casserole that it just fits, heat gently and brown the chicken for about 2–3 minutes, turning often. Add the stock or water, and bring to just simmering point. Cover and simmer gently for about 1¼ hours, turning the chicken over 2–3 times.
4 Add the olives, preserved lemon, cilantro, and parsley to the pan. Cover and cook for about 15 minutes until the chicken is very tender. Taste the sauce—if the flavour needs to be more concentrated, transfer the chicken to a warmed serving dish, cover and keep warm, and boil the cooking juices to a rich sauce. Tilt the pan and skim off any surplus fat, then pour over the chicken. Serve with couscous, if liked.

Serves 4
Preparation time: 20 minutes
Cooking time: 1¾ hours

CHICKEN ROLLS WITH LEMON, SAGE, AND WALNUT STUFFING

3 boneless, skinless chicken breasts, about 4 ounces each, halved
finely grated zest of 2 lemons
4 tablespoons fresh wholewheat breadcrumbs
I small onion, finely chopped
I tablespoon chopped sage
I tablespoon chopped walnuts
I egg white
⅔ cup Chicken Stock (see page 10)
⅔ cup fresh lemon juice
salt and pepper

To garnish:
sage sprigs
lemon wedges

1 Place the chicken breasts between dampened sheets of waxed paper and beat gently with a meat mallet or rolling pin.

2 Mix together the lemon zest, breadcrumbs, onion, sage, and walnuts. Season with salt and pepper and bind together with the egg white. Spread the mixture evenly over each chicken breast. Roll up securely and tie with fine string.

3 Put the chicken rolls in a shallow pan and add the stock and lemon juice. Cover, bring to a boil, and simmer for 25–30 minutes until the chicken is just tender.

4 Using a slotted spoon, transfer the chicken rolls to a serving dish, remove the strings, and keep warm. Boil the cooking liquid until reduced by half. Spoon the liquid over the chicken and garnish with sage sprigs and lemon wedges.

Serves 6
Preparation time: 20 minutes
Cooking time: 30–35 minutes

BROILED CHICKEN WITH WITH LEMON AND HERB MARINADE

4 chicken breasts, about 5 ounces each
cilantro sprigs, to garnish

Lemon and herb marinade:
grated rind and juice of 1 lemon
1 tablespoon olive oil
2 scallions, including 1 inch of green part,
finely chopped
1 tablespoon chopped thyme
1½ tablespoons chopped cilantro
¼ teaspoon ground coriander
salt and pepper

1 Put the chicken breasts in a single layer in a shallow non-metallic baking dish.

2 To make the marinade, mix together the grated rind and juice of the lemon, the olive oil, the chopped scallions, thyme, cilantro, ground coriander, and season with salt and pepper to taste. Pour over the chicken, cover, and refrigerate for 8 hours, turning occasionally.

3 Preheat the broiler to moderate.

4 Sprinkle salt over the skin side of the chicken and broil for 8–10 minutes until the skin is golden, brushing with any mixture remaining in the dish.

5 Turn the chicken over, sprinkle with salt, and brush with the cooking juices and remaining marinade mixture. Cook for a further 10 minutes or until the juices run clear. Serve garnished with cilantro.

Serves 4
Preparation time: 15 minutes, plus marinating
Cooking time: 18–20 minutes

CHICKEN WITH SAGE AND LEMON

**4 skinless chicken breasts, about
5 ounces each
5 tablespoons olive oil
3 tablespoons lemon juice
28 small sage leaves
3 tablespoons unsalted butter
salt and pepper
puy lentils, to serve (optional)**

1 Place the chicken breasts in a single layer in a non–metallic dish. Pour over 3 tablespoons of the oil and the lemon juice. Scatter over the sage leaves, turn the chicken so that the breasts are evenly coated, then cover and leave for about 30 minutes.

2 Lift the chicken breasts from the marinade and reserve the sage leaves separately. Pat the breasts dry. Strain the marinade into a small bowl.

3 Heat the butter and the remaining oil in a skillet, add the chicken, and cook for about 10 minutes over a moderate heat until browned. Turn the chicken breasts over, season with salt and pepper, and tuck the sage leaves around them. Cook for a further 10 minutes until the underside is brown and the chicken is cooked though.

4 Transfer the chicken to a warmed serving plate, then cover and keep warm.

5 Tilt the pan and pour off the fat. Place the pan over the heat and stir in the reserved marinade, scraping up any brown bits from the bottom of the pan. Boil until reduced to a brown glaze. Serve the chicken in slices, on a bed of puy lentils, if liked. Pour the remaining marinade over the chicken and garnish with the sage leaves.

Serves 4
Preparation time: 15 minutes, plus marinating
Cooking time: 20 minutes

LIME AND GINGER CHICKEN

4 chicken breasts, about 5 ounces each
I lime, halved and thinly sliced
I-inch piece fresh ginger, peeled and grated
2 tablespoons light soy sauce
2 tablespoons dry sherry
I red chile, seeded and finely sliced
flat-leaf parsley sprigs, to garnish
steamed vegetables, to serve (optional)

I Preheat the broiler to moderate.

2 Remove and discard the skin from each chicken breast. Make a few deep cuts through the meat, making sure not to cut all the way through the breast. Push a slice of lime into each slit and place the chicken on the broiler pan.

3 In a bowl, mix together the ginger, soy sauce, sherry, and chile. Brush over each chicken breast and leave to stand for 10 minutes.

4 Place the chicken under the broiler and broil for 20–30 minutes or until the juices run clear, covering the meat with foil if necessary to prevent it from over–browning. Warm the remaining marinade and drizzle over the chicken before serving. Garnish with flat-leaf parsley and serve with steamed vegetables, if liked.

Serves 4
Preparation time: 5 minutes, plus standing
Cooking time: 20–30 minutes

POACHED CHICKEN WITH LEMON SAUCE

3 lemons
3 tablespoons olive oil
3½ pound broiler-roaster chicken,
cut into pieces
3¾ cups Chicken Stock (see page 10)
3 egg yolks
⅔ cup sour cream
salt and pepper

1 Cut one of the lemons in half and rub over the chicken. Leave at room temperature for about 1 hour.

2 Heat the oil and fry the chicken pieces until browned, then transfer to a heavy, wide flameproof casserole. Pour over enough stock just to cover the chicken. Add salt and pepper, bring to just simmering point, cover tightly, and poach for 35–45 minutes until the chicken is very tender. Remove the chicken from the dish. Increase the heat underneath the casserole and boil the stock until reduced to about 1¼ cups.

3 Meanwhile, skin the chicken and remove the meat from the bones in large pieces. Add the skin and bones to the boiling stock and place the chicken on a warm dish. Cover and keep warm.

4 Squeeze the remaining 2 lemons. Blend the egg yolks with 5 tablespoons of lemon juice, then stir in the sour cream. Discard the skin and bones from the stock, then skim any fat from the surface. Lower the heat. Stir a few spoonfuls of the stock into the egg yolk mixture, then pour into the casserole. Cook, stirring, until lightly thickened, but do not allow to boil. Adjust the seasoning and lemon juice, if necessary. Pour some over the chicken and serve the remainder separately in a warmed jug.

5 To serve cold, place the cooked chicken as it is removed from the bones on a cold plate and leave to cool completely. Allow the sauce to cool completely, stirring frequently, then spoon over the chicken pieces.

Serves 4
Preparation time: 25 minutes, plus marinating
Cooking time: 1 hour

ASIAN CITRUS CHICKEN SKEWERS

I pound boneless, skinless chicken breast, diced

grated zest and juice of I lemon

2 tablespoons Chinese five-spice powder

I tablespoon dark soy sauce

julienned vegetables (carrots, scallions, radishes), to serve (optional)

1 Place the diced chicken, lemon zest and juice, five-spice powder, and soy sauce in a bowl. Stir to combine, cover, then leave to marinate in the refrigerator for at least 1 hour or overnight.
2 Preheat the broiler to moderate. Thread the chicken pieces on to 4 presoaked wooden skewers, packing them tightly together. Broil for 10 minutes. Turn the skewers, baste with any remaining marinade, and broil for a further 10 minutes. Serve on a bed of julienned vegetables, if liked.

Serves 4
Preparation time: 5 minutes, plus marinating
Cooking time: 20 minutes

TURKEY WITH COCONUT, GINGER, AND LIME

1 pound turkey breast fillets, cut into thin strips across the grain
2 tablespoons vegetable oil
1¼ cups coconut milk
juice of ½ lime
pepper

Marinade:
1-inch piece fresh ginger, peeled and crushed
1 garlic clove, crushed
finely grated zest and juice of ½ lime
2 tablespoons soy sauce
2 teaspoons light brown sugar

To garnish:
lime slices
chopped cilantro leaves

1 To make the marinade, mix all the marinade ingredients together in a shallow dish, add the turkey strips, and turn to coat. Cover and set aside for at least 20 minutes.

2 Heat a wok until hot. Add the oil and heat over a moderate heat until hot. Add the turkey and its marinade and stir-fry for 3–4 minutes or until lightly browned on all sides.

3 Add half of the coconut milk and bring to a boil, stirring, then stir-fry for a further 2 minutes.

4 Using a slotted spoon, remove the turkey from the sauce, arrange on a warmed serving platter, cover and keep hot.

5 Pour the remaining coconut milk into the wok, then add the lime juice. Increase the heat to high and bring to a boil. Stir for 2 minutes or until the sauce has thickened. Add pepper to taste, then pour over the turkey. Garnish with lime slices and cilantro leaves and serve immediately.

Serves 3–4

Preparation time: 10 minutes, plus marinating
Cooking time: about 15 minutes

PORK WITH LIME

**10 ounce loin of pork, cut into
1-inch x ½-inch strips
2 tablespoons light soy sauce
½ teaspoon ground black pepper
1 tablespoon oil
2 garlic cloves, chopped
3 small green chiles, chopped
4 tablespoons lime juice
4 tablespoons fish sauce (nam pla)
1 tablespoon jaggery or light brown sugar
2 tablespoons mint leaves, finely chopped**

1 Mix the pork, soy sauce, and pepper together in a bowl.
2 Heat a wok until hot. Add the oil and heat over a high heat until hot. Add the pork mixture and stir-fry, turning and stirring constantly, for 6 minutes or until the pork is well cooked.
3 Transfer the pork to a mixing bowl and add all the remaining ingredients. Mix thoroughly, then turn into a serving dish.

Serves 2
Preparation time: 10–12 minutes
Cooking time: 6 minutes

CITRUS PORK LOIN WITH OLIVES

¼ **cup butter**
I small onion, finely chopped
2¾ pound loin of pork
I½ tablespoons Marsala wine
juice of I orange
juice of I lemon
½ cup Chicken Stock (see page 10)
12 black Calamata olives, pitted and chopped
salt and pepper
roast pumpkin wedges, to serve (optional)
cilantro sprigs, to garnish

I Melt the butter in a large flameproof casserole over a medium heat, add the onion, and cook until golden but not brown. Add the loin of pork and brown it on all sides.

2 Add the Marsala and, when it has evaporated, the orange and lemon juices. Season with salt and pepper, cover, and cook over a low heat for about 1½ hours. Add a little stock occasionally to make sure it does not dry out.

3 Halfway through the cooking time, add the olives to the pork with a little pepper.

4 Serve the pork thinly sliced with the cooking juices poured over, accompanied by roast pumpkin wedges, if liked and garnished with cilantro sprigs.

Serves 6
Preparation time: 10 minutes
Cooking time: 1¾ hours

TAHITIAN LIMED FISH

I pound fresh fish fillets
2 limes
I tablespoon olive oil
6 scallions, sliced
2 tablespoons green peppercorns, lightly crushed
I head iceberg lettuce
2 canned pimientos, diced
salt and pepper
2 tomatoes, skinned and quartered, to garnish

1 With a sharp knife, cut the raw fish into very thin slices which are almost transparent. Pare the zest thinly from the limes and reserve. Squeeze the juice from the limes. Spread the fish slices on a chilled plate and drizzle over the lime juice.

2 Combine the olive oil, salt, pepper, scallions, and peppercorns. Sprinkle the mixture over the fish and leave to marinate for 1 hour. Cut the lime zest into julienne strips, drop them into boiling water, and blanch for 1 minute. Drain.

3 Make a bed of lettuce leaves on 4 plates and arrange slices of marinated fish on them with any of the remaining marinade. Scatter the blanched lime zest and pimientos over the fish and garnish with tomato quarters.

Serves 4
Preparation time: 15 minutes, plus marinating
Cooking time: 1 minute

SARDINES WITH LEMON AND PARSLEY

6 tablespoons olive oil
3 tablespoons lemon juice
2 tablespoons chopped parsley
2 pounds prepared fresh sardines
salt and pepper
lemon wedges, to garnish

1 Mix together the olive oil, lemon juice, and parsley. Season with salt and pepper.

2 Brush the mixture over the sardines and leave to marinate for 1 hour.

3 Preheat the broiler to moderate. Broil the sardines for about 2–3 minutes on each side, brushing with the lemon mixture as the fish browns and when turning it.

4 Serve with the remaining lemon mixture poured over the sardines and garnish with lemon wedges.

Serves 4
Preparation time: 5 minutes, plus marinating
Cooking time: 4–6 minutes

SEA BASS WITH LIME AÏOLI

4 large potatoes, unpeeled
4 tablespoons olive oil
4 sea bass fillets, 6–8 ounces each
salt and pepper

Lime aïoli:
4–6 garlic cloves, crushed
2 egg yolks
juice and finely grated zest of 2 limes
1¼ cups extra virgin olive oil

To serve:
grilled lime slices
snipped chives

1 Prepare the barbecue or preheat a grill pan.

2 To make the aïoli, place the garlic and egg yolks in a food processor or blender, add the lime juice, and process briefly to mix. With the machine running, gradually add the olive oil in a thin steady stream until the mixture forms a thick cream. Turn into a bowl, stir in the lime zest, and season with salt and pepper. Set aside.

3 Slice the potatoes thinly and brush well with olive oil. Sprinkle the slices with salt and pepper and place on the barbecue grill or on the grill pan. Grill for 2–3 minutes on each side or until tender and golden. Remove from the heat and keep warm.

4 Score the sea bass fillets, brush well with the remaining olive oil, and place them on the barbecue grill or on the grill pan, skin side down. Grill for 3–4 minutes until just cooked, turning once. Remove from the heat and serve with the potatoes and the aïoli and garnish with lime slices and snipped chives.

Serves 4
Preparation time: 30 minutes
Cooking time: 8–10 minutes

CRISPY LEMON FISH WITH MUSHROOMS AND SNOWPEAS

12 ounces monkfish tails, skinned and
cut into bite-sized pieces
2 tablespoons vegetable oil
2 tablespoons sesame oil
2 cups button mushrooms, sliced
2 cups snowpeas, tops removed
flat-leaf parsley, to garnish

Marinade:
1-inch piece fresh ginger, peeled and finely
chopped
1 garlic clove, crushed
3 tablespoons soy sauce
finely grated zest and juice
of 1 large lemon
½ teaspoon Chinese five-spice powder

1 To make the marinade, put the ginger, garlic, soy sauce, lemon zest and juice, and five-spice powder in a shallow dish. Add the monkfish and turn to coat. Cover and leave to marinate for about 30 minutes, turning the fish occasionally.

2 Heat a wok until hot. Add 1 tablespoon each of the vegetable and sesame oils and heat over a moderate heat until hot. Add the mushrooms and snowpeas and stir-fry for 3–4 minutes or until the juices run from the mushrooms. Transfer the vegetables and juices to a bowl and set aside.

3 Return the wok to the heat, add the remaining oil, and heat until hot. Using a slotted spoon, transfer the monkfish to the wok. Stir-fry for 5 minutes, then return the vegetables and juices to the wok and pour in the marinade. Increase the heat to high and toss until all the ingredients are combined and piping hot.

4 Serve immediately, garnished with sprigs of flat-leaf parsley.

Serves 3–4
Preparation time: 20 minutes, plus marinating
Cooking time: 12–13 minutes

CALAMARI WITH PEPPERS AND LEMON

I pound cleaned calamari
3 tablespoons olive oil
I red bell pepper, cored, seeded,
and chopped
2 garlic cloves, chopped
I dried red chile, crumbled
finely grated zest of I small lemon
3 tablespoons lemon juice
I tablespoon chopped parsley
salt and pepper
lemon wedges, to serve

I Chop the calamari tentacles roughly and cut the bodies into ¼–½-inch thick rings.

2 Heat the oil in a sauté pan or deep skillet, add the red bell pepper, garlic, chile, and lemon zest, and cook fairly gently, stirring occasionally, for about 5 minutes. Increase the heat to moderately high, stir in the calamari, and sauté for 1–1½ minutes until it becomes opaque and just tender.

3 Transfer the calamari to a warmed serving dish, sprinkle with lemon juice and parsley, and season with salt and pepper to taste. Serve immediately with lemon wedges.

Serves 4
Preparation time: 10 minutes
Cooking time: 6–6½ minutes

SCALLOPS WITH LEMON AND GINGER

1 tablespoon butter
2 tablespoons vegetable oil
8 shelled scallops, defrosted and dried
thoroughly if frozen, cut into thick slices
½ bunch scallions, thinly sliced diagonally
½ teaspoon turmeric
3 tablespoons lemon juice
2 tablespoons Chinese rice wine
or dry sherry
2 pieces stem ginger, with syrup, chopped
salt and pepper

1 Heat a wok until hot. Add the butter and 1 tablespoon of the oil and heat over a gentle heat until foaming. Add the sliced scallops and stir-fry for 3 minutes. Remove the wok from the heat. Using a slotted spoon, transfer the scallops to a plate and set aside.

2 Return the wok to a moderate heat, add the remaining oil, and heat until hot. Add the scallions and turmeric and stir-fry for a few seconds. Add the lemon juice and rice wine or sherry and bring to a boil, then stir in the stem ginger.

3 Return the scallops and their juices to the wok and toss until heated though. Season with salt and pepper to taste and serve immediately.

Serves 3–4
Preparation time: 10 minutes
Cooking time: 10 minutes

LEMON TART

This recipe is illustrated on page 2

Pastry:
1½ cups all-purpose flour
¼ teaspoon baking powder
pinch of salt
⅓ cup superfine sugar
finely grated zest of 1 lemon
½ cup chilled butter, diced
1 egg yolk

Filling:
2 eggs
2 egg yolks
¼ cup superfine sugar
4 teaspoons cornstarch
finely grated zest of 1 lemon
½ pint milk
½ pint heavy cream

To decorate:
lemon slices
confectioners' sugar

1 To make the pastry, sift the flour, baking powder, and salt on to a cold surface and stir in the sugar and lemon zest. Make a well in the center and put the butter and egg yolk into the well. Using your fingertips, gradually work the flour into the butter and egg yolk. Gather the dough together, then roll it out gently to a rough round on a floured surface. Lift the round into a 9-inch fluted tart pan with a removable bottom and press the pastry into the corners and up the sides with your fingertips. Trim the top edge with a knife, then chill in the refrigerator for 30 minutes.

2 Preheat the oven to 375°F. Prick the bottom of the pastry case all over with a fork, then line with foil and fill with baking beans. Place the tart pan on a baking sheet in the oven and bake blind for 15 minutes. Remove the foil and beans and set the pastry case aside, still on the baking sheet. Reduce the oven temperature to 325°F.

3 Meanwhile, make the filling. Put the eggs, egg yolks, sugar, cornstarch, and lemon zest in a bowl and whisk well to mix. Heat the milk and cream in a heavy saucepan until just below boiling point, then pour it into the egg mixture, beating constantly. Return to the pan and cook over a low heat until thickened, stirring constantly.

4 Pour the custard into the partially baked pastry case and bake for 30 minutes or until the filling is just set.

5 Leave the tart in the pan until lukewarm, then place on a serving platter. Serve warm or cold, decorated with lemon slices, with confectioners' sugar sifted over the top.

Serves 6
Preparation time: 30 minutes, plus chilling and cooling
Cooking time: 45 minutes

LEMON MERINGUE PIE

Pastry:
1½ cups all-purpose flour
6 tablespoons chilled butter, cubed
¼ cup superfine sugar
½ cup ground hazelnuts
1 egg yolk

Filling:
½ cup cornstarch
½ cup superfine sugar
1¼ cups water
grated zest and juice of 2 lemons
3 egg yolks

Meringue:
3 egg whites
¾ cup superfine sugar

1 To make the pastry, place the flour in a bowl, add the diced butter, and rub it in with your fingertips until the mixture resembles fine breadcrumbs. Stir in the sugar and ground hazelnuts, then add the egg yolk and 2–3 tablespoons cold water to mix to a firm dough.

2 Knead the dough briefly on a lightly floured surface, then roll out and line an 8-inch pie pan. Chill for 30 minutes, then line with foil and fill with baking beans.

3 Preheat the oven to 400°F. Bake the pastry case for 15 minutes, then remove the foil and beans and bake for a further 5 minutes.

4 Meanwhile, make the filling. Mix the cornstarch and superfine sugar in a saucepan. Stir in the water and lemon zest and juice until well blended. Bring to a boil, stirring until the sauce is thick and smooth. Cool slightly. Beat the egg yolks in a bowl, then stir in 2 tablespoons of the sauce. Return this mixture to the pan and cook gently until the sauce has thickened further. Pour the sauce into the pastry case.

5 Beat the egg whites in a grease-free bowl until they are stiff and dry. Beat in 1 tablespoon of the sugar, then fold in the remainder. Spread the meringue over the filling to completely enclose it.

6 Return the pie to the oven for 10 minutes until the meringue is golden. Serve warm or cold.

Serves 8
Preparation time: 25 minutes, plus chilling
Cooking time: 35–40 minutes

KEY LIME PIE

Pie crust:
1¾ cups graham cracker crumbs
2 tablespoons superfine sugar
6 tablespoons butter, melted

Filling:
3 eggs, separated
14-ounce can sweetened condensed milk
½ cup freshly squeezed lime juice
1 tablespoon lemon juice
2 teaspoons grated lime zest
2 tablespoons superfine sugar

Topping:
1 cup heavy cream
1 tablespoon confectioners' sugar
few drops of vanilla extract
lime slices, to decorate (optional)

1 Mix together the graham cracker crumbs, sugar and melted butter and press over the bottom and up the sides of a 9-inch springform pan. Refrigerate while making the filling.

2 Lightly beat the egg yolks together until creamy. Add the condensed milk, lime and lemon juices and lime zest and beat until well mixed and slightly thickened.

3 In another bowl, make the filling. Beat the egg whites until frothy. Add the sugar and continue beating until the meringue holds soft peaks. Fold gently but thoroughly into the lime mixture using a large metal spoon.

4 Preheat the oven to 325°F. Spoon the filling into the crumb crust and smooth the top. Bake in the oven for 15–20 minutes or until the filling is just firm and lightly browned on top. When cool, refrigerate the pie for at least 3 hours, until it is well chilled.

5 To make the topping, whip the cream until it begins to thicken. Add the sugar and vanilla extract and continue whipping until quite thick but not stiff. Spread the cream over the top of the chilled pie. Decorate with twisted lime slices, if liked. Remove the side of the pan just before serving, and serve well chilled, decorated with lime slices, if liked.

Serves 8
Preparation time: 30 minutes, plus chilling
Cooking time: 15–20 minutes

BAKED LEMON AND BAY CUSTARDS

12 bay leaves, bruised
2 tablespoons grated lemon zest
⅔ cup heavy cream
4 eggs
1 egg yolk
⅔ cup superfine sugar
scant ½ cup lemon juice

1 Put the bay leaves, lemon zest, and cream in a small saucepan and heat gently until it reaches boiling point. Remove from the heat and set aside for 2 hours to infuse.

2 Beat the eggs, egg yolk, and sugar together until the mixture is pale and creamy, then beat in the lemon juice. Press the cream mixture through a fine sieve into the bowl and stir until well combined.

3 Preheat the oven to 225°F. Pour the custard equally into 8 individual ramekin dishes and place on a baking sheet.

4 Bake for 50 minutes or until the custards are almost set in the middle. Leave to cool and chill until required. Return to room temperature before serving.

Serves 8
Preparation time: 10 minutes, plus infusing and chilling
Cooking time: 55 minutes

MANGO AND LIME SHERBET

1 large ripe mango
2 tablespoons lime juice
⅔ cup sour cream
2 egg whites
¼ cup superfine sugar
lime slices, to decorate

1 Hold the mango over the bowl of a food processor or blender. Cut the mango into quarters, reserving the juice in the bowl below. Cut away all the flesh from the stone. Scrape the flesh from the skin of the mango into the bowl.
2 Place the lime juice and the sour cream in the food processor or blender and blend to a purée. Transfer the mixture to a freezer container.
3 Put the egg whites in a bowl and whip them until they form soft peaks. Add the sugar, 1 teaspoon at a time, beating constantly. Fold the egg mixture into the mango mixture and freeze until firm without further beating.
4 Serve in chilled glasses and decorate with lime slices.

Serves 4–6
Preparation time: 10 minutes, plus freezing

GIN AND LIME SORBET

⅓ cup granulated sugar
2½ cups water
1 lime, thinly peeled
3 tablespoons lime juice
3 tablespoons gin
2 egg whites
lime slices, to decorate

1 Put the sugar, water, and lime peel in a small heavy-based saucepan and stir over a low heat until the sugar has dissolved. Bring the mixture to a boil and let it bubble up for 10–15 minutes until it has reduced by half. Set aside to cool.
2 Squeeze the juice from the lime and add it and the gin to the mixture. Chill in the refrigerator, then strain into a freezer tray and freeze for about 1 hour until partially frozen.
3 Beat the egg whites until stiff, then fold them into the chilled mixture and freeze until set.
4 Serve in chilled glasses and decorate with lime slices.

Serves 4–6
Preparation time: 10 minutes, plus cooling and freezing
Cooking time: 15–20 minutes

LEMON AND HONEY ICE

4 large or 6 medium lemons
about 4 tablespoons water
2 tablespoons clear honey
¼ cup superfine sugar
I bay leaf or I lemon balm sprig
2 cups natural yogurt or
fromage frais
strips of lemon zest, to decorate

1 Slice off the top of each lemon. Carefully scoop out all the pulp and juice with a teaspoon. Discard any white pith, skin, and pits, then purée the pulp and juice in a food processor or blender. You will need ⅔ cup. If there is less than this, top it up with water.

2 Put the water, honey, sugar, and bay leaf or lemon balm into a saucepan. Stir over a low heat until the sugar has dissolved, then leave to cool. Blend the mixture with the lemon purée and the yogurt or fromage frais. Do not remove the herb at this stage.

3 Pour into a freezer tray or shallow dish and freeze until lightly frozen, then gently fork the mixture and remove the herb. Return the ice to the freezer.

4 Transfer the ice to the refrigerator about 20 minutes before serving. Serve decorated with strips of lemon zest.

Serves 4–6
Preparation time: 20–25 minutes, plus cooling and freezing

LEMON AND POLENTA SYRUP CAKE

This recipe is illustrated on page 3

¾ **cup butter**
¾ **cup superfine sugar**
I **cup ground almonds**
⅓ **cup flaked almonds**
½ **teaspoon vanilla extract**
2 **large eggs**
finely grated zest and juice of I lemon
¾ **cup polenta flour**
½ **teaspoon baking powder**

Syrup:
grated zest and juice of 2 lemons
¼ **cup superfine sugar**
2 **tablespoons of water**

I Preheat the oven to 350°F. Line a 8½-inch cake pan with baking parchment paper.
2 Beat together the butter and sugar until light and creamy. Add the ground and flaked almonds, vanilla extract, and eggs and mix well. Add the lemon zest and juice, polenta, and baking powder and mix well. Spoon the mixture into the prepared pan and bake for 25 minutes.
3 Meanwhile, make the syrup. Put the lemon zest and juice, superfine sugar and water in a saucepan and heat through. Spoon over the cake as soon as it comes out of the oven. Allow the syrup to drizzle through. Serve the cake hot or cold.

Serves 4–6
Preparation time: 10 minutes
Cooking time: 25 minutes

LEMON BUTTER COOKIES

I **cup butter**
grated zest of I lemon
I **cup granulated sugar**
2 **cups flour, sifted**

I Beat the butter with the lemon zest until creamy. Add the granulated sugar and beat well. Stir in the flour. Cover and chill for 30 minutes.
2 Preheat the oven to 350°F.
3 Take teaspoonfuls of the mixture and roll lightly into balls. Place on ungreased baking sheets and press down with a fork which has been dipped in cold water to prevent sticking. Bake for 10–12 minutes or until slightly browned.
4 Transfer the cookies to a wire rack. Cool and store in an airtight tin until required.

Makes about 50
Preparation time: 15 minutes, plus chilling and cooling
Cooking time: 10–12 minutes

CARROT AND LIME CAKE

⅔ cup Lime Marmalade (see page 58)
2 tablespoons freshly squeezed lime juice
2½ cups finely grated carrots
I cup raisins
½ cup unsalted butter, softened
½ cup light brown sugar
2 eggs
2 cups superfine self-rising
wholewheat flour

Topping:
⅔ cup low-fat cream cheese
2 teaspoons clear honey
I tablespoon lime juice
I tablespoon shredded lime zest

1 Preheat the oven to 325°F. Grease and line the base of a 9-inch round springform pan. Heat the marmalade and lime juice together in a small saucepan until the marmalade has melted. Remove the pan from the heat and stir in the carrots and raisins. Leave to cool.

2 Place the butter and sugar in a large mixing bowl and beat together with a wooden spoon until light and fluffy. Add the eggs, one at a time, beating well after each addition until the mixture is thick and smooth.

3 Pour the cooled carrot mixture into the mixing bowl and add the flour, carefully folding it in with a spatula until evenly blended.

4 Spoon the mixture into the prepared pan, level the top, and bake in the center of the oven for about 1 hour or until the cake springs back when the center is lightly pressed.

5 Loosen the edge of the cake with a palette knife and release the pan. Remove the base and paper and leave the cake to cool on a wire rack.

6 To make the topping, beat the cream cheese, honey, and lime juice in a bowl. Spread the topping evenly over the top of the cake and decorate with lime zest.

Serves 8–10
Preparation time: 20 minutes, plus cooling
Cooking time: 1 hour

LIME OR LEMON MARMALADE

16 medium limes or 8 large lemons, zest removed and cut into fine shreds
8 cups cold water
4 pounds sugar

1 Remove the white pith and place on a square of clean muslin. If using limes, discard the pits; if using lemons, add the pits to the pith. Tie the muslin loosely. Chop the flesh finely.
2 Put the rind, flesh and juice, muslin bag, and water in a pan. Bring to a boil and simmer for 2 hours, until reduced by half.
3 To test for pectin, put a teaspoon of the mixture on a saucer. When a firm clot is obtained, discard the muslin bag.
4 Weigh the pulp and add 1 pound of sugar for each 1 pound of pulp. Heat gently, until dissolved, then bring to the boil and boil rapidly until setting point is reached. This can be tested by cooling a teaspoon of marmalade on a saucer. A skin should form which wrinkles when pushed with a finger.
5 Remove from the heat and skim off any scum. Leave for a few minutes, stir again and pour into hot sterilized jars. Put in waxed discs immediately. Cover when cold.

Makes about 6 pounds
Preparation time: 20 minutes
Cooking time: about 2½ hours

SCOTTISH LEMON CURD

3 large lemons
¾ cup unsalted butter
1 pound sugar
4 eggs, beaten
3 tablespoons Drambuie

1 Grate the rind from the lemons using a fine grater.
2 Melt the butter slowly in a heavy-based saucepan and stir in the lemon rind and sugar. Heat gently until the sugar has dissolved.
3 Stir 1 tablespoon of the hot mixture into the beaten eggs. Repeat two more times as this prevents the eggs curdling.
4 Pour the mixture into the pan and heat gently, stirring, until the mixture thickens and coats the back of a wooden spoon. Stir in the Drambuie and heat until thick again. Do not boil. Pour into hot sterilized jars and cover.

Makes about 1½ pounds
Preparation time: 10 minutes
Cooking time: about 30 minutes

LEMONADE ON THE ROCKS

6 lemons
2½ cups water
½ cup superfine sugar

To serve:
crushed ice
chilled still or sparkling mineral water

To decorate:
lemon slices
mint sprigs

1 Grate the zest from the lemons—be careful to take just the zest and none of the white pith. Squeeze the lemon juice into a jug and reserve. Pour the water and sugar into a large saucepan and add the lemon zest. Stir until the sugar has dissolved, then boil for 5 minutes. Leave to cool, then stir in the lemon juice.

2 To serve, strain a little lemonade into glasses or into a jug. Add crushed ice and top up with chilled mineral water. Decorate with lemon slices and mint sprigs.

Serves 6
Preparation time: 10–15 minutes, plus cooling
Cooking time: 8–10 minutes

LIMEADE

6 limes
½ cup superfine sugar
3 cups boiling water
pinch of salt
ice cubes
mint sprigs, to decorate

1 Halve and squeeze the limes into a large jug, then put the squeezed halves into a heatproof jug with the sugar and boiling water. Leave to infuse for 15 minutes.

2 Add the salt, stir the infusion well, then strain it into a jug with the lime juice. Add 6 ice cubes, cover and refrigerate for 2 hours or until cold.

3 To serve, place 3–4 ice cubes in each glass and pour the limeade over them. Decorate with mint sprigs.

Serves 6
Preparation time: 6 minutes, plus infusing and chilling

ICED MINT TEA

12 mint sprigs
1 large lemon, finely chopped
1 tablespoon sugar
4 cups tea, strained
ice cubes
lemon slices, to decorate

1 Chop 4 of the mint sprigs and put them into a large heatproof pitcher with the chopped lemon and sugar. Pour over the tea and allow the mixture to infuse for about 30 minutes. Strain into another pitcher and chill until required.

2 To serve, pour into glasses filled with ice cubes and decorate each glass with lemon slices and 2 of the remaining mint sprigs.

Serves 4
Preparation time: 5 minutes, plus infusing and chilling

LONG ISLAND ICED TEA

To make sugar syrup, put 4 tablespoons superfine sugar and 4 tablespoons water in a saucepan.
Bring to the boil, then boil for 1–2 minutes. Leave to cool.

6 ice cubes
¼ fluid ounce gin
¼ fluid ounce vodka
¼ fluid ounce white rum
¼ fluid ounce tequila
¼ fluid ounce Cointreau
1½ fluid ounces lemon juice
½ teaspoon sugar syrup
cola, to fill
lemon slice, to decorate

1 Put the ice cubes into a mixing glass. Add the gin, vodka, rum, tequila, Cointreau, lemon juice, and sugar syrup. Stir well, then strain into a tall glass almost filled with ice cubes.

2 Fill with cola and decorate with the slice of lemon.

Serves 1
Preparation time: 5 minutes

DAIQUIRI

¾ cup cracked ice
1½ fluid ounces sugar syrup
(see Long Island Iced Tea)
2¼ fluid ounces lime juice
9 fluid ounces rum

Shake all the ingredients well in a cocktail shaker and strain into chilled glasses.

Serves 4
Preparation time: 5 minutes

MARGARITA

lime juice
coarse salt
¾ cup cracked ice
8 fluid ounces tequila
2¼ fluid ounces lime juice
½ fluid ounce triple sec
finely grated lime zest, to decorate

Rub the rims of the glasses with lime juice and then spin them in salt. Shake all the remaining ingredients well in a cocktail shaker and strain into the glasses. Decorate with lime zest.

Serves 4
Preparation time: 5 minutes

CUBA LIBRE

2–3 ice cubes
2¼ fluid ounces dark rum
juice of ½ lime
cola, to top up
slice of lime, to decorate

Place the ice cubes into a tall tumbler and pour over the rum and lime juice. Stir to mix. Fill with cola, decorate with a slice of lime, and drink with a straw.

Serves 1
Preparation time: 3 minutes

TEQUILA SUNSET

4–5 ice cubes
1½ fluid ounces gold tequila
7½ fluid ounces fresh lemon juice
1½ fluid ounces fresh orange juice
2 tablespoons honey
crushed ice
lemon zest spiral, to decorate

Put the tequila into a chilled cocktail glass, add the lemon juice and then the orange juice and stir. Drizzle the honey into the glass so that it falls into a layer at the bottom of the glass, add the crushed ice and decorate with a lemon zest spiral.

Serves 1
Preparation time: 4 minutes

INDEX